The True Meaning of Christmas

Written by John & Irene Lynch
Illustrated by Daniel Oviedo

The True Meaning of Christmas
Copyrighted ©2021
Irene Lynch

Published by Lynch Legacy
ISBN: 978-1-7361183-4-4 (Paperback)
ISBN: 978-1-7361183-5-1 (Hardcover)
Printed in the United States

Cover Art & Illustrated By: Daniel Oviedo

All rights reserved. No part of this publication may be reproduced, stored in a retrieval system, or transmitted in any form or by any means-electronic, mechanical, photocopying, recording, or otherwise without the prior written permission of the publisher and copyright owners.

This book is dedicated to our grandchildren:

Jack, Gracie, A.J., Brooklyn, and Carson.

May you always look at life through the eyes of a child and believe in the true meaning of Christmas.

Christmas was coming, and A.J. and Brooklyn could not wait. The smell of pine from the Christmas tree was in the air in their house. Each ornament sparkled from the reflection of the lights on the tree. Presents were neatly wrapped and under the tree. A.J. and Brooklyn were getting ready to visit their grandma and granddad's house to decorate gingerbread houses. Decorating gingerbread houses was a favorite tradition that happened every year. They were especially excited because their cousins Jack and Gracie always joined them, and this year their youngest cousin, Carson, would be there too!

They walked into their grandparents' house to the sounds of Christmas music and the squeals of excitement from their cousin, Carson. Gracie hugged Brooklyn and Jack gave A.J. a fist bump.

Grandma and Granddad's house was decorated for Christmas. There was a large wreath with red balls and lights on the front door. A Christmas tree was in their living room and was decorated with lights, ornaments, and tinsel. Presents were wrapped and placed underneath the tree. Stockings were hung on the fireplace mantel, and a wreath with four candles was placed on top.

A.J. asked, "What is that Grandma?" pointing to the wreath. Grandma said, "It is an Advent wreath." Jack and Gracie knew what it was and said they have one at their house. Grandma told A.J. and Brooklyn that it was to help them prepare for the birth of baby Jesus.
"We love God by preparing for Christmas during Advent. This is a time when we go to church, pray, and prepare," said Grandma.

Each Sunday starting with the Sunday after Thanksgiving, Grandma lit one of the candles. Three of the candles were purple, and one was pink. Grandma said the first candle that she will light is purple. It represents hope. On the second Sunday in Advent, she will light another purple one. It represents faith. The third Sunday in Advent is when the pink candle will be lit and is called Gaudete

Sunday. It represents joy! On the fourth and last Sunday of Advent, Grandma will light the last purple candle to represent peace. She said that during the four weeks leading up to Christmas, we are to pray and prepare for the coming of the baby Jesus.

Grandma brought the children over to the large round dining room table. It was covered with the best decorations for the gingerbread houses.

There were green and red sprinkles, colored gumdrops, candy canes, marshmallows, pretzels, M&Ms, white frosting, coconut flakes, and peppermint candies to put on all the gingerbread houses.

This year there will be five houses to decorate, one for each of the children!

Many candy pieces never made it onto the gingerbread houses as the giggling children quickly ate them. The children covered the bases with white coconut flakes to make a snow scene.

Laughter could be heard as each grandchild decorated their unique gingerbread house.

Granddad helped with putting the houses together. Grandma supplied the bottom of a box for each one to have a safe carrying display to place their gingerbread houses.

When they were finished with their gingerbread houses, the children were hungry. Granddad bought pizza, and Grandma provided the festive Christmas paper plates, milk, and ice cream for dessert.

After the gingerbread houses were made and everyone had eaten, Grandma baked Christmas cookies, and the children helped. They made butter cookies cut into stars, bells, wreaths, and angels using a cookie cutter, and Gracie and Brooklyn decorated some with red and green sprinkles. A.J. and Jack placed tiny colored candy beads on the cookies they were decorating while Carson looked on and laughed. The smell of homemade cookies filled the air. Grandma promised everyone a bag of cookies to take home.

When the children were eating their Christmas cookies, Grandma showed them her manger display. She told them that she had always had one in her house at Christmas time. It represents the day baby Jesus was born.

She pointed out Jesus' mother and said, "This is the Blessed Mother, Mary. Mary is Jesus' mother. Jesus wanted to share her with all of us, and He gave her to be our mother, too". She then pointed out the figure next to Mary and said, "This is Mary's husband, St. Joseph, who raised Jesus. He was a carpenter and a holy man."

There were animals near the baby Jesus, and Grandma said, "Jesus was born in a manger with the animals to show us humility. He is a king and our God, but He came to live among us."

There were three other statues. Each one wore a crown or royal robe. Grandma said they were the three wise men who came looking for Jesus to bring Him gifts.

Grandma said that Christmas is Jesus' birthday. Our celebration is really a birthday party for the baby Jesus!

A.J. asked Grandma, "Why do we give each other gifts if it is Jesus' birthday?"

Grandma smiled and said, "Jesus wants everyone to love one another! He gave us this commandment",

"A new commandment I give to you, that you love one another: just as I have loved you, you also are to love one another. (John 13:34-35 ESV-CE)."

"We love one another when we give to the poor, give gifts of love, spend time with family and friends, and be kind to one another. Christmas is a special time to show love, although we should do it all year long!" Grandma said with a smile.

After a long and fun day, the grandchildren went home to their parents, proudly carrying their gingerbread houses.

On the following Sunday, everyone was together again at church. In the foyer, as they were leaving, Grandma saw the Giving Tree. It looked like a Christmas tree, but instead of glass ornaments, it had paper ornaments with gift requests printed on them. These requests were for gifts to help families in need, nursing homes patients, foster children, and anyone who needed help buying Christmas gifts this year. Grandma took five ornaments off the tree.

She said, "I'm taking one for each of my grandchildren. I'm going to buy five presents because God has blessed me with five beautiful grandchildren." When A.J. and Brooklyn heard her say this, they smiled.

Grandma said she would shop with Granddad for the presents that week and bring them back to the church next Sunday so that the church volunteers could sort them by the label on the tag and distribute them the week before Christmas.

"Look, Grandma, this boy is my age, and he wants a game!" exclaimed A.J. when he saw one of her tags. "This girl is my age, and she wants a doll!" Brooklyn shouted.

Grandma said, "Do you two want to help me pick out these gifts? We can go to the toy shop this week." They shouted, "Yes!"

A.J. and Brooklyn thought about the girl and the boy opening the presents they would pick out. They also thought of all the people opening presents on Christmas day because of the love of strangers.

They understood what Grandma meant when she said, "Jesus said to love one another. This is our birthday gift to Him."

About the Authors

John and Irene Lynch are husband and wife and reside in Sarasota, Florida. "*The True Meaning of Christmas*" is their third children's book. They co-wrote and published "*The Legend of the Tooth Fairy*" and "*Can We Have a Puppy?*"

John Lynch taught elementary school students in grades second through sixth for forty-one years before retiring in 2013. He taught at the Balch School in Norwood, Massachusetts, for sixteen years before moving to Sarasota, Florida, with his family. John taught at Ashton Elementary School for seventeen years and eight years at Tatum Ridge Elementary School in Sarasota, Florida.

Irene Lynch retired as an educator in 2013. She taught kindergarten and first grade at Philippi Shores Elementary School. She was a resource teacher and Exceptional Student Education Liaison at Fruitville Elementary, an assistant principal at Venice Middle and Sarasota Middle School before becoming Epiphany Cathedral School's principal in Venice, Florida.

They are spending their retirement years writing children's books with the assistance of their grandchildren!